GK'S POETIC MIND

TRULY POETIC

GARVIT KHURANA

Dedicated to my Pet budgies :

To Happy and Canary who are the stars of my eyes

To My lovely Cookie in the heaven above

And to Sunshine and Lemon who are with god.

Contents

Contents

Foreword

It gives me immense pleasure to know that my student Garvit Khurana is aspiring to become a budding writing. He is a briliant child ready to face challenges in every field of life.

At such a young age, he is setting an example of self confidence and dedication. He is a respectful and sincere student, ready to help his classmates. He is much aware of his capabilities and is responsible enough to be called an ideal student.

His writing reveals his love for nature and his understanding of human psychology. He seems to have a passion for Science as a subject which is clearly revealed in one of his poems- 'Wondrous Science' and also for Mathematics, which he remarks- is a game.

I request the readers to understand the depth of his writings and encourage this budding artist to work better and attain success in life.

- Mr. Gavin Bond

Preface

Greetings to the reader of my book....

It was in 2018 when I first wrote a rhyme. My second one was in 2020 while I was in class 7 but I never had the realisation of my poetic mind before I was in class 9 in 2022. I started poetry as a passion on the last pages of my school diary and here I am now, penning down my first book. I am currently 14 as I write this book and am currently studying in class 9 at St. Xavier's School in Chandigarh.

I really hope that this book I have written with honest and nature loving thoughts appeals to you and enlightens you in some way or the other. The poems are mostly related to Nature and how the humans are destroying it, planning their own extinction. There are some poems that you might find relatable and funny while some relate to School and study. I hope you enjoy this journey into my Poetic mind.

Thanks,

Garvit Khurana

Author

Acknowledgements

First of all, I would like to thank the Almighty, Guru Nanak Dev Ji to give me the strength and thoughts to write this book.

I am grateful to my grandparents Bodh Raj Khurana and Satya Khurana, my parents Tarun Khurana and Monika Khurana, my younger brother Arshit Khurana who is the source of my motivation and my friends who provided me with their full fledged support and guidance.

I would specially like to thank my teachers Mr. Gavin Bond and Mrs. Kavita Sodhi from St Xavier's Sr. Sec. School Chandigarh and Ms. Pooja Singh, my batch mentor.

1. Poetic Mind

If love for nature you show
You have a heart which is kind
What is creative in you
Is your Poetic Mind

If words you can properly rhyme
By taking a walk ideas you find
What pens poems on paper
Is your Poetic Mind.

The pure thoughts you get
With love they are bind
What represents you hobby
Is your Poetic Mind

If you can express your thoughts
In words of such kind
What helps you think
Is your Poetic Mind

Understand the hidden meanings
No one else can find
What makes you different
Is your Poetic Mind

A liking expressed
For sentences that bind
What brings you close to poetry
Is your Poetic Mind

The language of love
Is one of its kind
What makes you poetic
Is your Poetic Mind.

I wish by my heart
Interesting enough you find
What helped me write this book
Is my Poetic Mind

2. Green Life

A person who plants a tree
Plants a gift for the world and thee
Takes a step for making free
The Earth of pollution and impurity
A person who plants a tree
Plants a gift for the world and thee.

He is a Noble Man
The one who plants a tree
He is a man of God
Who saves the world from fie
A person who plants a tree
Plants a gift for the world and thee.

Green Palms waving in the breeze
And mangoes with fruits on them in counts of ten.
The beautiful flowers around the trees
Sadness from us they seize
So beautiful are the trees which wave and sing.
Chirps of birds in our ears ring

O' we feel so stress free
A person who plants a tree
Plants a gift for the world and thee.

It's our duty
To preserve the worlds beauty
So pure, of the blossoms
Is the scent we get.
Carry on like this
And the Earth will be gone, I bet.
If we stop polluting and spreading impurity
Then only the Earth be
Of its all troubles free
A person who plants a tree
Plants a gift for the world and thee.

Image Source : Canva

3. Stressed at School

While work kept mounting high,
Eager he was to say good bye,
To the school for the day and the friends that lie
The day went slow, Slow as an injured snail would go.
But still it ended as a relief,
He was cool, once at home like a coral reef.
It had been like robbing a bank
The day ended, He did thank.

Image Source : Canva

4. True Good Deeds

There is not a bigger joy
Than feeding the birds
Not a scene more satisfactory
Than seeing the grazing herds

Serving nature
Seems so kind
Can empower vision
Of even the blind.

The chirps of the sparrow
And the white dove
The fights of the crows
Show the natural love.

The way they eat,
And the way they sing,
Life seems so good,
As of a king.

Be Peacock or Raven
From the Kingdom of aves
All are parts of nature
May live in jungles or caves.

My activity diurnal
For the nature, it's my duty
Feeding the fliers of the sky,
Preserving the natural beauty.

A perch coloured grey,
With Food and water
Extends a few birds' life
Which otherwise would have been shorter.

The love on the face,
Of a dog stray
If we just feed them
With heart for us they pray.

They are happy

And love the human souls,
Grateful, protecting for them
Loyal more than a 100 moles.

By bringing back our morals
We can become humans again
If we become Kind and Positive
And not be selfish for our gain.

Think and Ponder
Of how shall earth be revived
Get Ideas for wonder
Or we shall be despised.

Think before polluting
And think before killing
If birds and animals disappear,
We shall suffer what we are not willing.

The last thing to say
About this noble thing
Preserve what we are losing
And be the miraculous king.

Save the world
By saving the critters
And we shall rejoice,
By eating some fritters.

Image Source : Canva

5. Earth Day

The home in which we are born
The only planet which life exists on,
We are children of the earth
The place where we took birth.
O' people, come and celebrate
Earth day has come.

We got a problem, Earth's got a cure
But is it happy, are we sure?
Earth gives us so many things
But are we good human beings
Why are we not keeping our home clean?
Why is it full of repulsive filth and cans of tin?

We should now shake our hands
And let dreams; the truth become
O' people come and celebrate
Earth day has come.

6. Burn it

This Diwali, burn it
Burn it as much as you can
Burn the ego in you
Not the crackers, as they give the Earth a tan
Don't be so rude, don't be a selfish man
Burn the ego in you
Not the crackers, as they give the Earth a tan.

The Earth gives us everything we need
But in return, what do we feed
We feed pollution and chemical solution
And fulfil our greed
So, This Diwali, burn it
Burn it as much as you can

Be a good plant, not a forest weed
All will throw you when you are of no need
Show some care and not your greed
So, burn the ego in you
Not the crackers as they give the Earth a tan

GARVIT KHURANA

This Diwali burn it, burn it
Burn it as much as you can
Don't be so greedy
Be a good man.

Image Source : Canva

7. Exam

What every student does fear
It is what they hate to hear.
Scared from it, Staring at a palm
That frightening thing is exam.
Destroys the weather which is calm
Children regard it as the biggest harm,
To cancel their trip to a lovely farm
The hated thing is exam.

Toppers, average and children who sit on back benches,
Feel as if they are in the trenches.
All of them, in stress
Troubled of this monster, heads pressed
Brains confused, failing guessed.

Toppers unstatified, with their high percentile.
Averages happy, with the marks they thought they got
By walking a hundred miles.
Backbenchers grateful that they passed,
This hard time at least surpassed.

Parents angry and they advance,
To scold children, they get a chance.
Failiures cry and toppers dance
For ten days atleast, they change their stance.
It also changes the flavour of food,
Low scorers confused, Toppers in attitude.
But atleast it ended
Pains in some time will be mended.
Everyone is grateful, that they can rest and sit by a palm
Happy it ended, this was exam.

Image Source : Canva

8. Inhuman

Today I saw a dog, Defending its owner
Then I saw two men, Fighting with each other
I thought of something while standing near the oven.
Animals are caring, Humans Inhuman.

We have lost love, and respect.
We think selfishly of caste and sect.
Beings we are, the most advance
But to be called human, we lost the chance.
Trees give us life,
Due to nature, we survive. But we destroy them and they don't
revive.
And destroying nature, in happiness we thrive.
Cold we are, as a cry of a Raven,
Plants are giving, humans inhuman.

Loyalty of Dogs, is a true example.
Humans betray, proofs are ample
Animals love, statement simple.
Humans fight and cheat,

Even for a little bun
Animals are loving, humans inhuman.

We cut trees, don't grow more
Destroying the nature for sure,
We got issues, nature's got a cure
We have a heart, which is not pure.
Our mind's got selfish. We are now blind
Continue like this no forest you'll find
No nature left, everything will bind.
After so much cruelty
They say nothing and work gets done
Nature is caring, Humans Inhuman.

The world will end, the thoughts will bend.
We will realize, that we are wrong.
Extinction will knock, ding-dong.
Save the Earth, Save yourself and be sure.
Remember,
Precaution is better than cure.
Nothing left, Extinction done and
Then our souls will say
Nature was protecting, Humans inhuman

Image Source : Canva

9. Dominance that Destructs

The Arrogance of a human,
Has become a trend.
Like this, we continue to run
And the world will end.

We Terminate animals,
For our selfish act.
We are nobody but criminals
Of extinction, we're signing a pact.

We are uprooting every Holt,
Breaking what we should mend
Closing the chest of Oxygen, by locking the bolt
We are walking towards the end.

We show dominance,
Over animals and twigs.

By showing our false prominence
We are cursed by fauna and trees of figs.

For our selfish way of survival,
Through workshops and industries
Making the nature our rival,
Forcing it towards unwanted disabilities.

We've not left a place
Without pollution and trash,
By infecting space,
We move towards our crash.

The nature gives us everything,
And what do we provide?
Let's restore this lovely thing,
Because what don't wait, are time and tide.

A step towards golden tomorrow,
Save the world from fie.
Regret for this old sorrow,
And we will be free, so will thee.

10. Novel Journey

Day was warm
Ac was on
I was bored and tired
Thought I'd watch some TV
But the idea got fired
When I saw along with a chess rook
A light green Ruskin Bond book.

That's when it started
My love for books
The curiosity of mystery
What happened to the crook?
The hero's new look
And the friendly new cook
That was when I read my first novel book.

Then it went on and on
And the count reached thirty
I grew keener to know
What happened to Berty?

Then entered 'Roald dahl'
With his little Charlie
Increasing count of books
With the speed of a Harley.

Then came the best day
The cane was cut shorter
The beautiful day when I got Harry Potter
I read and read and read
And read in dreams when I was in bed

The best book on Earth,
The mysteries to which it led
And after seven of them
Voldemort was dead.
Finishing sequels, I read prequels
And re-read the legendary eight times along with some lime
And never did it happen; the curiosity did sublime
And keenness grew for some
Adventures of crime.
Literally Seventy
The number grew
As I read about a Pirate's crew.

My love for books is always
And I advise you too
Books add wisdom to knowledge
You will acknowledge.
Try and love books and you will be too.

Image Source : Canva

11. Something Short... Something Special

Earth is the planet best
We are worsening it then the rest,
We think this is a funny jest,
Why we are doing is the quest
Destroying a little bird's nest
Celebrating destruction as a fest.

From the east and to the west
We are sour as a lemon zest
We fail in the humanity test
And are now like a dirty pest.

We are cruel and we are dumb
And we'll be cursed for what we do and not by the Nature blest,
We will realise when destruction shows,
How we stabbed Earth through the Chest,

12. Prototype

A machine of metal
As Large as a kettle
With a boy, it did settle.
Feelings in that child,
It made ripe
and it was called a Prototype.

The boy grew up with it
With it he shared his stationery kit.
It was his only friend,
His starting of life and the end.
It played with him and taught him how to snipe,
And it was called a Prototype.

It was built for study
of a fellow buddy.
His Phsycology and thought
What in his brain he got.
It listened to all his gripe
And it was called a Prototype

With the innocent child it played,
For him, with him he always stayed.
He loved him more than a human could
For him he could eat hard raw wood
And cared for him, like one should.
It seemed the little robot, had come from heaven
Made the boy's life, a peacock,s from Raven.
The Little boy's tear, It did wipe
And It was called a Prototype.

A Better model made, of beautiful look
The notice of our robot, now nobody took,
They forgot him, head they shook.
The boy and the robot cried, as if they had almost died
and sadly survived.
After such sacrifices, and learning of emotions
He was forced to hear, such bad notations.
Humans don't value love, they just talk tripe
Divine this angel was and it was called a Prototype.

The boy was the only one, who understood
With the company of great, atleast he was good.
Without his mother, Life was unclear

And all that helped, was a robot peer.
He lived with it the whole life.
The life without him would have been a mountain sheer,
The one who wiped his every single tear.
He tried to make humans improve
With love as water in a hose pipe
This unvalued loveable Robo, it was called a Prototype.

Image Source : Canva

13. Thoughts and Actions

What we think,
And what we do differ,
We act misjudged
And then we suffer.

We think of our world,
Restored to health
But what we do is
Greed for wealth

We guys complain
That the birds don't fly,
But with our actions
Do our thought comply?

We want the forest
Full of horses and colts,
But where will they go,
If we burn all the Holts.

Who doesn't wish for animal survival !
But still hunting is a popular sport.
We plan the future
While our sail drowns near the port.

Who think we are the only good,
Calling the others mad,
Who are we to do so?
The ones who can't differ in good and bad.

Why break the animal's home
Why stop them from taking rest,
Just don't trouble them
And You'll be blest.

The Lovely nests of the birds,
Are the symbols of life,
Why destroy the pure objects,
Why stab your life with a knife.

We need to change these thoughts of ours,

Make them practical from dumb
Save the nature and save the Earth
Is like the assuring sign of a thumb.

If we don't transform,
We shall pursue the sin
Save nature to save yourself
Or get killed by the cold within.

Image Source : Canva

14. Wondrous Science

Science,

The subject best.

Easily, it beats the rest.

Bio, Physics and Chemistry

Seem interesting, its history

Gives logic for every mystery .

Everything to something does comply,

Tells you even how flies a fly.

Physics tells you logic

For every motion and momentum,
All problems solved not some
Once you understand it, you always hum.
To calculate you have numericals
Which do seem like miracles
What happens and how, It will tell you the best
Start studying physics, and it'll do the rest.

❧❧❧

Chemistry full of reactions and Carbon isotopes
Study it properly
For good marks, it brings up the hopes.
Hundred's of exceptions, do seem wild
Sulphuric Acid Strong, Hcl is mild.
Good for the studious but a nightmare for an average child.
Your marks are not fluttery, if you study chemistry

❧❧❧

Structures of cells and diagrams'
Study of seeds, maize and grams.
Microscopes and specimens
Do seem really interesting
Scores get high, if you understand
Topper you'll be, if you don't cram.
You'll be a great buddy
Biology, if you study.

❧❧❧

Studies are great, So is science
So intelligent you'll be,
of Newton and Einstien you'll show the signs.
There's nothing you'll find illogical, dear buddy
Science is wondrous, if you study.

15. The Crescent of Colors

The Seven Colors of the Rainbow
Are a wonderful sight
So true the meaning they show
All they tell is right.

White scatters the hue
And symbolises unity
As pure as the morning dew
As long as together, we have dignity.

The Color vibrant 'Red'
Represents sacrifices of the brave
To give tribute to the dead
And walk on the way they pave.

Orange the Color of pride
Of bravery it is the crest

Keep your heart open and wide
And of love you'll have a full chest.

Yellow shows the crops
Grown by honest farmers
They fulfil the family stocks
And feed the ones in armours.

The green represents earth
And its lovely woods
It shows our place of birth
And the natural hood.

The blue speaks for marine
And the aqua beasts
The seas ultra-sheen
As royal as a priest.

Indigo is for the midnight sky,
And the shining stars
Time to bid work good bye
And resting time for cars.

Violet is for imagination
Shows the life advance
The development of every nation
The deserving get the chance.

The Colors of the rainbow
For our safety, assure
For nature love you show
and good health is sure.

16. Mathematics

A tool highly used,
Maths it has the name.
Stats and calculations
Is what inside this game.

Students imagine horror,
As if maths will hypnotise
Bullies us to solve its problems
From air which seems to rise

In units like trigonometry
Are sin, cos and tan,
With their reciprocals
It is simply hard for a man.

Now numbers and letters
Why do they confuse
When it's about algebra
I wonder where I can use.

Of quadrilaterals and triangles
Areas you have to find,
Formulas like Herons' gave
Really blow up the mind.

Lines, angles and polygons
Line segments and rays
With congruency and similarity
To confuse there are multiple ways.

The maths that is commercial
Is no use for science.
For interest compound and simple
Just make it to pies of mince.

The subject is interesting enough,
To success it paves the ways
Just follow the rules and logically reason.
And do as the BODMAS says.

Mathematics

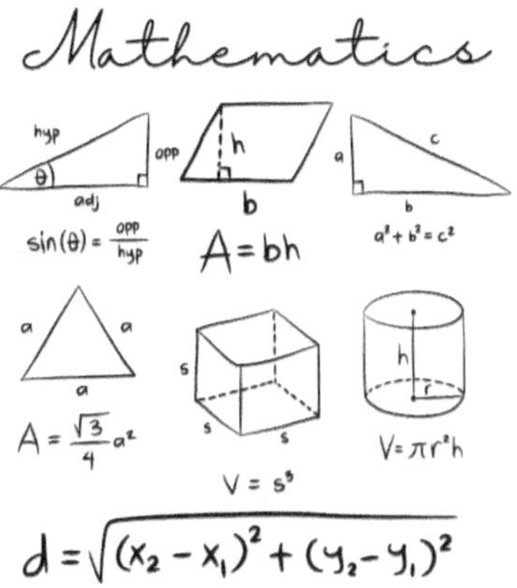

Image Source : Canva

17. Suicide

By creating our own destroyers
Towards darkness we ride
By making tech smarter than us
We commit Suicide

As we create AIs
And Robots of good quality,
We send our fellows
Towards sadness and poverty.

Things become techy
All become advance
For aspirants who're worthy
There is left- no chance.

We make IT dominated
By our own creation.
We destroy oppurtunities
For students from every nation.

With these inventions
Unemployement will increase
Creativity will go down
Economy will decrease

If everybody is fallen
In the poverty pit
How can one use such tech
If they can't afford it.

The intelligence of our mind
And its creations are the king
But what is such a creation for
If it drains up everything

Use technology wisely
Computers were made by us
Let them not replace humans
Or our future will be suss.

One thing is to be added

Respect the ones alive
May it be animals or plants
In this pool of new era tech, Be cautious before you dive.

Be careful, be wise
And keep your mind wide
By letting technology dominate
Do not commit suicide

18. The Two sides of Cold

Warmth of the fire
With cold does abide
Opinions do matter
For a coin doesn't have one side.

Cold is liked
By some worldly folks
The cozy bonfires
On which their chicken smokes.

Food and quilts,
Are good when combined
As satisfying as if
A big diamond is mined.

Some people on this Earth,
Find the cold as bitter.
Want it to go quickly
As quick as kids spread litter.

The absence of sunlight
Is what they complain,
Having a life lazy,
Is what seems their pain.

Thought are thoughts
Positive we should think,
Importance it has
Fire, food, sun and a blanket mink :)

Image Source : Canva

19. The Printing Press

Rivalry, the reason for
The stupid act of Artillery war,
No side wins and the innocent fall
A printing press prints it all.

The destruction that happens
Dead daughters and dead sons,
For a stop to war they call
A printing press prints it all.

People starved and unfed
Makes the nature ridden at bed
While poor die, Rich horrify the public hall
A printing press prints it all

Destructed economy, and the wasted land
Makes the world desolated, as a desert full of sand,
Dismantling the world, end is on the Scroll,
A printing press prints it all.

Money is wasted, resources drown
People who just fight, for entire lives they frown,
Go on like this, to end we all will crawl
A printing press prints it all.

The envy between two sides
To heaven the soldier rides,
As the rate of death gets tall,
A printing press prints it all.

Life of people war destroys
And of Little girls and boys.
Still a great fight they call,
A printing press prints it all.

Thinking of the fool,
To take the war as cool.
These are the ones who become a loll
A printing press prints it all.

Bieng with the worldly will

GARVIT KHURANA

Peace is not what we should kill
Humanity to the world, Reinstall
A printing press prints it all.

Understand the loss,
Let's repair all the flaws,
Preserving the Earth, Is the dutiful call,
A printing press prints it all.

Image Source : Canva

20. Nation

What I feel proud of
It is my first passion
Always loyal to it
It is my nation

The Golden bird of history
Of cultures it's the base
The land's diversity
Of India this is the praise.

Power of my country
The British had oppressed
For freedom of this nation
Everybody had stressed

In the year 1947
Independence we won
In this race of nations
With high speed we run

The development to the world
The great Indians brought
Every second company
A CEO Indian sought

The Inventions and studies
Our Scholars unveiled
These are the basis of everything
We excel in every field

Relations we maintain
With countries all around
If you come to India
Generosity will be found

Our flag tricolour
Represents Integrity
The pride of our Nation
It represents unity

The land that grows gold

Fertility it has the best
Our country is our life
Of love it is the crest.

The rivers, the forest
And the desert of Thar
The landforms so glorious
And our ocean that stretches so far

Of trade and cultures
India is the king
In dance we are superb
Awesome when we sing

The beauty of our nation
Is too sweet and sound
Anybody who comes
In India's love is bound.

Our Spices and textiles
And the varied flavours of food
Are the best in the world!
Always enlighten your mood.

Of love we are the followers
By God India is blest
With its beautiful traditions
Our country is the best

The people of our country
And their language verified
Respect each other
And with Secularism abide

Bharat, Aryavarta and India
It is called by many names
The land of varied cultures
Where originated plays and games.

Hail my nation
To India I salute
This land where I am born
To existence it did prelude.

21. The Face of a destroyed world

A dark Aura everywhere
Humanity Erased
Fire all around
Destruction the planet faced

Buildings fallen
And property drains
As the fire spreads
The gibbous moon wanes

No more humans
Animals and plants
No one is to be seen
Not even spiders and ants

Imagination of such scene
Is too hard for us men

But do we realize
With our activities, our own death we pen

At the rate we are going
We plan our extinction
To the existence of life
We give zero contribution

We kill, we cheat
We pollute and hurt
We are the nasty creatures
Who convert life to dirt!

Us the humans great
Picture our glorious win
But we destroy our planet
By committing every sin

By hearing the words so harsh
Our ears seem to pain
The transition to death
Is our thirst for gain.

We should improve ourselves
Still there is time
We can control this
Or the Earth will sublime

This is to understand
Think on a sofa…curled
The face that I the ugliest
Is of a destroyed world

Image Source : Canva

22. The World I Imagine

The World I imagine
Greenery everywhere
Where polluting is called a sin
This is the face of the world
Which I imagine

Roads with clean sides
And trees all around
Birds flying in the skies
And no trash stacked mound

Where nature is at its best
And humans are united
Where animals are respected
And where they seem delighted

Where there is love for every being
Discrimination out of mind
Where helping is the duty

No one is left behind

The Forest spread everywhere
And wild life is preserved
Where lands not for factories
But for biospheres reserved

Where global warming is a history
Ozone is restored to health
The world will be the best
When humanity is the real wealth

Where water bodies are pure
And the marine have free will
Where mountains are clean and
No trash is there on the hill

Species where diverse
In population thick resides
The Rule of Respect
With love we all abide

GARVIT KHURANA

Imagining such a world
Is a wondrous thought
We all come together and
A big change is brought

A request of the nature
Let this dream become reality
Let the world heal
And we end this cruelty

Image Source : Canva

23. A walk in my lawn

An experience of immense pleasure
In my lawn when I take a walk
Life at its best it seems
To stress it puts a lock.

The place is where I am in thoughts
Its aura hypnotising
The positivity I sense and
The flowers mesmerizing

The mat of grass green,
So soft when I take a step
Seems as good as
Topping the class without a prep.

The palms that wave in the breeze
Are like joy to stop the tears
The chirps of the sparrows
Are like music to my ears

When I look at the fruits
And the freshness of the flowers
My mind is most relaxed
I seem to have all powers

When I take a round
Of the vegetable patch
I feel full of satisfaction
Illness as they snatch

The vegetables organic
Provide me with good health
The crops that grow in the ground
Notify of the real wealth
Ideas I get
This garden does inspire
Improves the air around
In which we respire

It accelerates my brain
To the speed as same as a blink
For poetry it promotes

My poetic mind to think.

Image Source : Canva